CORNERSTONES OF FREEDOM™

THE FRENCH REVOLUTION

BY JOSH GREGORY

CHILDREN'S PRESS®

An Imprint of Scholastic Inc.

New York   Toronto   London   Auckland   Sydney
Mexico City   New Delhi   Hong Kong
Danbury, Connecticut

BRINGING HISTORY to LIFE

Content Consultant
James Marten, PhD
Professor and Chair, History Department
Marquette University
Milwaukee, Wisconsin

Library of Congress Cataloging-in-Publication Data

Gregory, Josh.
 The French Revolution / by Josh Gregory.
  pages cm.—(Cornerstones of freedom)
 Includes bibliographical references and index.
 ISBN 978-0-531-28203-8 (lib. bdg.) — ISBN 978-0-531-27668-6 (pbk.)
 1. France—History—Revolution, 1789–1799—Juvenile literature. I. Title.
 DC148.G69 2013
 944.04—dc23   2013000076

1 2 3 4 5 6 7 8 9 10 R 23 22 21 20 19 18 17 16 15 14

Photographs © 2014: AP Images: 7, 8 (North Wind Picture Archives),
30 (Thibault Camus); Art Resource/RMN-Grand Palais: back cover;
Bridgeman Art Library: 16 (Louvre, Paris, France/Giraudon), 15, 56 top
(Musee de la Chartreuse, Douai, France/Giraudon); Getty Images: 18
(Apic), 54 (DeAgostini), 50 (English School), 12 (Hulton Archive), 4 bottom, 38; Library of Congress: 6, 25, 27; Shutterstock/Doug Stacey, Inc.: 5
bottom, 48; Superstock, Inc.: cover (Album/Prisma/Album), 13, 56 bottom
(Bridgeman Art Library), 41, 46 (ClassicStock.com), 31, 44 (DeAgostini),
14, 36, 47, 57 (The Art Archive), 19, 32, 35 (Universal Images Group), 2, 3, 4
top, 20, 22, 24, 40, 55, 58, 59; The Image Works: 10, 49 (Mary Evans Picture
Library), 5 top, 28 (Roger-Viollet).

Did you know that studying history can be fun?

BRING HISTORY TO LIFE by becoming a history investigator. Examine the evidence (primary and secondary source materials); cross-examine the people and witnesses. Take a look at what was happening at the time—but be careful! What happened years ago might suddenly become incredibly interesting and change the way you think!

Contents

Changing Times

The French writer Voltaire, whose real name was François-Marie Arouet, was one of the best-known voices of the Enlightenment.

Throughout the 1600s and 1700s, a new way of thinking began to sweep across Europe. During this period, known as the Enlightenment, writers and thinkers promoted the idea that people should rely on reason and logic rather than simply follow tradition or religion. They argued that reasonable people should educate themselves and seek freedom and happiness. As these notions spread, many people began thinking critically about their governments and religions. Some began to imagine a world in which rich, poor, noble born, and common people were treated more equally.

In 1776, these ideas were put to the test. British colonists in North America rose up against the government in England and declared themselves an independent nation. Europeans followed the news as the colonists defeated the British and formed a new nation called the United States. Many people in France—especially the poor and middle class—watched with great interest as the Americans freed themselves from the rule of a king and established a government where the people chose their own representatives.

From 1775 to 1783, American colonists battled against Great Britain in the Revolutionary War.

OFFICIALLY CONCLUDED IN 1783.

CHAPTER 1

THE MASSES REVOLT

French nobles lived lives of leisure and luxury that contrasted starkly with those of the lower classes.

As THE PEOPLE OF THE NEWLY formed United States were deciding how their new government would work, the French were experiencing a period of general unrest. The country's people were heavily divided by class. At the top of society were royalty, nobles, and leading members of the **clergy**. Though these people made up only a very small portion of the population, they held almost all of the nation's power and influence. The middle class, or bourgeoisie, was made up of merchants, business owners, and other professionals. While many of these people enjoyed comfortable incomes, they were largely prevented from having influence in the country's government. Peasants and other poor workers made up France's lower class. These people had almost no power over their lives and lacked any voice in government.

A Growing Dissatisfaction

As the end of the 18th century drew near, the limits caused by France's uneven class divisions combined with Enlightenment ideals to bring about widespread frustration with the country's leadership. The bourgeoisie, who made up a larger portion of the country's population than the nobles, were forced to pay far more taxes than people in the upper classes. At the time, the government offered them no way of changing this. France had been a **monarchy** for hundreds of years. Its king was free to create laws, appoint officials, and govern as he saw fit. The Catholic Church and the country's nobles held some influence, but the king had the final word in all legal matters.

The clergy of the Catholic Church held a great deal of power in French society around the time of the revolution.

France's peasants also had plenty of reasons to be unhappy. They had long labored as part of a system based on **feudalism**, common in Europe's Middle Ages. Wealthy members of the upper class owned the farmlands that peasants worked on. Though the peasants earned very little money from this work, they had to pay significant fees to the landowners. They were rarely allowed to purchase land for themselves. Almost all land was held by members of the upper class. The Catholic Church alone controlled 10 percent of the nation's land.

New Knowledge

Throughout the 18th century, the bourgeoisie had grown wealthier than ever before. This afforded them comfortable lifestyles, with plenty of leisure time to spend reading and socializing. In addition, more and more books and newspapers were being printed in France. Many of these publications bore the mark of the Enlightenment. A group of French writers known as the *philosophes* (philosophers) were among the most prominent thinkers of the Enlightenment. Among them were such great minds as Voltaire, Jean-Jacques Rousseau, and Anne-Robert-Jacques Turgot. The philosophes often wrote in support of major political, social, and **economic** reforms. They believed that people should desire a voice in their government and that all people should be equal.

Such ideas made perfect sense to a population that was unhappy with its leadership. The works of the philosophes were read widely among the French

Peasants performed long hours of difficult labor in France's fields, but saw little reward for their hard work.

middle class, who often came together to discuss news and politics. Such discussions spurred the spread of discontent among the populations of large cities such as Paris. Little by little, the ideals of the Enlightenment began to spread into the countryside, where peasants were eager to hear of a new way of thinking about society and their place within it.

Lacking Leadership

Under the rule of King Louis XVI, France was experiencing serious economic problems. The country had started supporting the colonists in the American Revolution in 1778. It provided large numbers of troops and supplies to its American allies, helping win the war while running up significant expenses. The U.S. government, still establishing itself, could not afford to repay the debt. At the same time, in part because of a refusal to tax members of the nobility, the government was not making enough money from taxes. The country was spending more than it took in. As a result, the French government found itself running very low on money by the mid-1780s.

This problem was made even worse by the king's habit of spending large amounts of money on his family's lavish lifestyle. His wife, Marie-Antoinette, was known throughout the country for her expensive tastes and uncaring attitude toward the country's poor.

Marie-Antoinette was descended from a long line of European nobles.

King Louis XVI

King Louis XVI was born on August 23, 1754, in Versailles, France. Taking the throne at the age of 19, he was seen as an immature leader who lacked confidence and was unable to make strong decisions.

As revolutionary attitudes spread throughout France, Louis neglected to take action to solve the crisis. Instead of working to reach a compromise with the people, he spent his time on hobbies such as hunting and lock making. This weak leadership and refusal to confront problems would eventually lead to his and the entire French monarchy's downfall.

Many people began to openly doubt the king's leadership abilities and economic choices. As the French lost confidence in their ruler, so did many foreigners. Other nations, and even private French investors, began refusing to give loans to France's government, making its financial situation even worse.

In addition, the 1780s saw major agricultural problems in France. Droughts led to poor harvests, and outbreaks of disease among livestock led to a decrease in available meat and dairy products. Food prices shot up, forcing much of the country's lower class to go hungry. With so many things going wrong all at once, tensions began to rise among the nation's common people.

A Failed Compromise

By the late 1780s, the French government realized that it would need to make changes to avoid losing control of the country's people. In August 1786, Charles-Alexandre de Calonne, France's controller general of finances, developed a plan for economic reform that he hoped would solve the country's financial problems while compromising with the middle class on tax issues. According to Calonne's plan, nobles would start paying taxes and give up certain privileges in return for having more influence in creating laws.

Calonne knew that his plan would meet with strong resistance from the upper class. He was especially concerned with the *parlements*,

Charles-Alexandre de Calonne was known among France's leaders as a financial genius.

the country's court system. Magistrates, who were the leaders of the parlements, often abused their power and refused to obey national laws. Many were corrupt and more concerned with preserving their own positions than with governing fairly. In an attempt to prevent the magistrates from rejecting his ideas, Calonne formed an Assembly of Notables. The assembly was made up of magistrates and other members of the upper class, including nobles and clergy. Calonne hoped to convince the assembly to agree to his plan in the interest of preserving the nation.

However, many assembly members were unwilling to pay the taxes that the plan would require of them. They

The parlements, which served as France's court system, were plagued with corrupt leadership.

did not think they should have to give up their privileged status. Calonne's plan failed, and Louis removed him from his position as controller general the following year.

Trouble in Paris

The country's financial situation continued to worsen as unrest approached a tipping point in large cities. This tension was especially strong in Paris, the nation's capital. With a population of around 600,000 people, the city was home to everyone from the poorest members of the working class to the wealthiest nobles. As a result, class differences were on clear display for anyone to see. As a laborer struggled to feed his family in a time of rising food prices, he could see rich people comfortably traveling through the city in fine clothing and carriages. Such an environment served to highlight the unfairness of the social and economic systems that had driven the country for centuries. By 1788, dissatisfaction among poor workers and peasants in Paris had led to a wave of rioting and looting. The same issues soon began plaguing other cities as well.

The Estates-General was meant to provide fair representation for all of France's social classes.

The Estates-General

In late 1788, King Louis called for an assembly of the Estates-General, a group of elected representatives that met during difficult times to give the country's people a voice in the government. It had no real power to make or change laws. Instead, its representatives presented the people's feelings and ideas to the king, who could then use this information to make his decisions.

Each of the three "estates" of French society were represented in the Estates-General. The clergy and the nobles made up the first two, while the Third Estate consisted of the country's bourgeoisie and peasant classes. Between January and April 1789, elections were held across the country to choose the representatives. The First and Second Estates were each allowed 300 representatives, while the Third Estate elected 600.

Each of the three estates worked together to create documents called *cahiers de doléances*. The cahiers were lists of complaints that each group had with the country's situation, as well as proposed methods for solving these issues.

SPOTLIGHT ON

The Estates-General

The Estates-General was a group of political representatives in France. It was assembled for the first time in April 1302 (shown above) to give King Philip IV advice in his feud with the Catholic pope. In the following decades, there were several more meetings, but these became less common over time. Government leaders considered the process of gathering the representatives together to be a troublesome and inefficient way of making decisions. The three estates often had difficulty agreeing, just as they did in the 1789 assembly, because each group had such different interests. By the 1500s, the Estates-General assembled only in times of great need, and 1614 marked the last time it would be called to gather until 1789.

Hundreds of National Assembly members swarmed King Louis's tennis courts and swore to remain there until they had created a new constitution.

The elected representatives met on May 5, 1789, in Versailles to begin discussing their ideas. The king and other government officials were also present to oversee the proceedings. Unfortunately, the plan did not go as smoothly as Louis had hoped it would. The three estates clashed almost immediately and spent more than a month arguing over the method of voting they would use. The clergy and nobles wanted to vote by estate. This would give them an advantage, as they could simply outvote the Third Estate two to one on any issues. The Third Estate proposed they should vote by person, which would give it the advantage because of its greater numbers.

An Assembly Forms

The king, supposedly in charge of the proceedings, could not control the representatives. Because it represented around 95 percent of the country's population, the Third Estate decided on June 17 that it had the right to proceed without the other two estates if a decision could not be made. The 600 middle- and lower-class representatives named themselves the National Assembly and demanded cooperation from the clergy and nobles. Most of the clergy and a few nobles were soon persuaded to join them. Royal officials, in an attempt to assert the king's authority, locked the newly formed assembly out of the Estates-General meeting room three days later. This inspired the representatives to take over the king's tennis courts, where they swore to remain until they had drawn up their own **constitution** for the country.

By June 27, Louis knew he was defeated. He agreed to give the National Assembly control over the country's reforms and encouraged the remaining nobles of the Estates-General to cooperate. On July 9, the National Assembly became the National Constituent Assembly. It did not represent three separate estates, but instead the entire population of France together as one. Louis was unhappy with the situation but realized that there was little he could do for the time being.

CHAPTER 2

NEW DIRECTIONS

King Louis XVI was widely seen as an ineffective ruler.

DESPITE LOUIS'S ACCEPTANCE of the Third Estate's demands, the lower classes remained distrustful. No sooner had the National Constituent Assembly established itself than panic began sweeping through the streets of Paris. This period, known as the Great Fear, was driven by widespread rumors that the king was working with the upper class to forcefully overthrow the increasingly powerful Third Estate. Protests and marches against the king became common, and the city's large peasant population grew fearful that the king would unleash the military on them.

Ninety-eight protesters were killed during the storming of the Bastille on July 14, 1789.

Storming the Bastille

As the peasant protest in Paris grew louder and angrier, the military was sent to ensure that large-scale violence did not break out. However, the appearance of French military forces around Paris only stoked the fires of the Great Fear. The protesting masses began to gather weapons in anticipation of battle. They opened the doors of many of the city's prisons, freeing the prisoners to fight with them against the government. On July 13, they raided military barracks to arm themselves with guns. However, they lacked the gunpowder needed to fire the weapons.

The following morning, a horde of protesters approached the massive Bastille prison. Behind its walls were more guns and a large supply of gunpowder. The protesters hoped to convince the prison governor to simply give them what they wanted. At 10:00 a.m., a small group of protesters was allowed inside to speak with the governor. Outside, the crowd of nearly a thousand people began to grow restless.

Around an hour after sending in their representatives, the protesters outside launched an attack on the Bastille. Some attacked guards and stormed through the

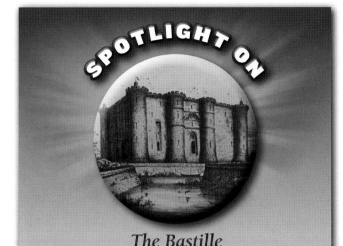

SPOTLIGHT ON

The Bastille

By the time the revolutionaries stormed its walls in 1789, the Bastille had long loomed over Paris as a reminder of royal power. King Charles V had wanted a fortress that could be used to defend the walls of Paris from attackers, so he ordered its construction in 1370. Later kings continued to improve and reinforce the Bastille. In time, it was turned into a prison. By 1789, the Bastille consisted of eight towers, each one 100 feet (30 meters) tall, with stone walls of the same height standing between them.

Soon after the storming, the new government ordered that the Bastille be torn down, completing the symbolic destruction of the king's power that the revolutionaries had begun.

fortress gates, while others began climbing the 100-foot (30-meter) walls. Soon, they had overtaken the Bastille, securing the ammunition they had come for. They also released the seven prisoners held inside.

Rising Up

After taking the Bastille, the protesters were swept up in a wave of revolutionary spirit. They began targeting other government institutions. As they moved through the city, they took aim at anything and anyone they believed to be standing in the way of freedom and equality. The revolutionaries beat and killed government officials, including the governor of the Bastille and the mayor of Paris. They continued to gather weapons and support, and soon controlled the entire city.

As these events unfolded, the revolution spread into the countryside. Inspired by the success of the revolutionaries in Paris, the peasants decided it was time to end the feudal system. In the following weeks, peasant farmers launched violent uprisings against the nobles who owned the lands. These protests began to frighten even the bourgeoisie, who wanted to see major government reforms. Back in Versailles, the National Constituent Assembly quickly voted to end the feudal system, knowing that it was the only way to stop the peasant uprisings. Approved on August 4, the assembly's declaration freed the peasants from the payments they had long been forced to surrender to landowners.

A Declaration of Rights

Twenty-two days after ending the feudal system, the assembly made another major move with the Declaration of the Rights of Man and of the Citizen. This document was similar to the United States' Declaration of Independence and outlined the assembly's goals of securing liberty and equality for all French people. Heavily inspired by Enlightenment thinkers such as Jean-Jacques Rousseau, the declaration's 17 articles provided a framework for the new French government.

The first article stated the document's main idea, that all "men are born and remain free and equal in rights." The second article specified that these basic rights included "liberty, property, security, and resistance to

The Declaration of Independence officially announced the North American colonies' separation from Great Britain.

oppression." Article six guaranteed that all citizens, not just members of the upper class, would be allowed to hold government positions. Other articles guaranteed the rights to free speech and freedom of religion. Importantly, the declaration required all citizens to pay taxes and required all laws regarding those taxes to be determined by elected officials.

While the declaration did not specifically call for an end to the monarchy, it severely limited the king's powers and was designed to prevent government officials from abusing their positions. It also broke down the country's rigid class barriers. This marked a major change from traditional French society. King Louis saw this as too much of a challenge to his position. He

The 17 articles of the Declaration of the Rights of Man were adopted between August 20 and August 26, 1789.

refused to endorse either the August 4 declaration to end the feudal system or the August 26 Declaration of the Rights of Man. Several Parisians responded to his refusal by marching to his home in Versailles, about 12 miles (20 kilometers) away. There, they forced the royal family to accompany them back to Paris.

Louis's refusal to approve these declarations was of little concern to the assembly. With the king now in Paris, he had no choice but to pay attention as the assembly set to work on a new constitution. It would be based on the ideals in the Declaration of the Rights of Man.

A New Political Climate

Though the king was still part of the government, he was now under the control of the National Constituent Assembly. Many people embraced the leadership of the assembly as it worked to develop a system of government that would allow elected officials to operate alongside a king.

Members of the bourgeoisie and peasant class—thrilled that they could now choose officials to represent them in the government—took a great interest in politics. Those who could read enjoyed books and newspapers, and everyone took part in active discussions. Many people joined political clubs where they could discuss their ideas about government with like-minded members. These clubs had names such as the Jacobin Club, the Club of the Cordeliers, and the Club of the Feuillants. Each had its own unique goals and priorities for governmental and social change. For example, the Jacobins focused on equality among all people, while the Cordeliers empha-

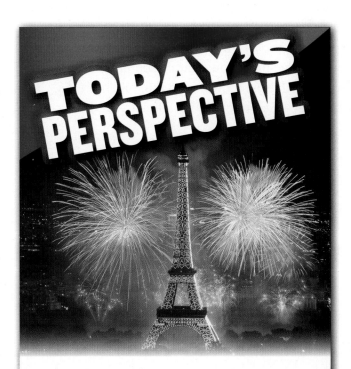

TODAY'S PERSPECTIVE

Since 1880, July 14 has been celebrated each year in France as Bastille Day. It is one of the country's biggest holidays. The festivities commemorate the day that the people of Paris rose up against the monarchy and began the French Revolution, changing the country forever.

Similar to Fourth of July celebrations in the United States, Bastille Day is often a time for huge fireworks displays and parades. Many people throw large parties.

A huge celebration in Paris marked the first anniversary of the fall of the Bastille, beginning a long tradition of commemorating the day.

sized eliminating religion and using the military to spread revolutionary ideas into other nations.

Regardless of their individual beliefs, most French people at the time celebrated the revolution. One year after the storming of the Bastille, a huge crowd came together in Paris to commemorate the anniversary with a feast. Others held ceremonial plantings of cypress trees, or "trees of liberty."

At the same time, the assembly continued to make changes to the old ways of doing things. To pay off part of the massive debt the country still held, it sold off the vast land holdings of the Catholic Church to the people. This raised funds while allowing more people to own land. The assembly also divided the nation up into smaller sections, each with its own local elected government.

The Counterrevolution

King Louis, meanwhile, continued to be unhappy with the direction the country was taking. On June 20, 1791, he attempted to flee with his family to Austria, but they were caught and returned to Paris. The Jacobins, led by National Constituent Assembly member Maximilien de Robespierre, called for Louis to be removed from

The Jacobin Club was also known as the Society of the Friends of the Constitution.

the government after the incident. Despite this, many members of the assembly continued to make sure the king retained a role in France's government.

On September 3, 1791, the assembly adopted the constitution it had been working on for two years. This new constitution established a form of government called a constitutional monarchy. Under this system, elected officials would be in charge of creating and changing laws, while the king had **veto** power and could appoint certain offices.

This compromise angered Robespierre and other more **radical** political figures. They believed strongly that the government should be chosen entirely by the people and that there was no room for a king in a truly free country.

They were not the only ones unhappy with the progress in France. Some of the country's citizens, almost all of them nobles, had opposed the revolution from its start. They knew it would bring an end to their privileged status. Many of them had fled to foreign nations when the revolution began. These people were known as *émigrés* (emigrants). Once they were safely across the borders, they attempted to drum up foreign support for a counterrevolution.

At first, the émigrés had little luck. European leaders were not concerned with the French Revolution in its early years. However, throughout 1791, many revolutionaries called for using the military to spread revolution throughout Europe. Even Louis was in support of this idea. He believed that a successful war might allow him to regain some control of the government, and a failed war would allow his foreign allies to help him escape from France.

An Outbreak of War

Louis's attempted escape from Paris earlier had made it obvious to other European rulers that the French king was not happy. Between this and the growing threat of a French invasion, European leaders became much more concerned with the events in France. In late 1791, nearby Austria and Prussia officially declared that they did not support France's revolutionary government. In reaction, France declared war on Austria, one of Europe's most powerful **empires**, on April 20, 1792.

The war did not start out well for France. In the first few months, it lost battle after battle to Austria's larger military. The uneven troop numbers were skewed further when Prussia allied with Austria in July. To make things worse, many of France's experienced military leaders had left the country as émigrés, leaving the military in the hands of inexperienced officers. Before long, the combined forces of Austria and Prussia had broken through into French territory, aiming to take Paris.

Many people blamed these losses on Louis, whom they believed to be working secretly against his own country. On August 10, a mob of angry Parisians surged into the palace where the royal family was staying, and captured them. The mob imprisoned the family in the Temple, an old fortress and prison that had been built in Paris in the 12th century.

At the Battle of Valmy, French generals Charles-François Dumouriez and François-Christophe Kellermann successfully commanded their forces against an army of Prussian invaders.

On September 20, the French military finally managed an important victory with the Battle of Valmy, to the east of Paris, preventing the Prussians from overrunning the French capital. This inspired the National Convention, which had replaced the National Constituent Assembly, to meet later that day. This group of 749 elected officials began discussing a major change for the government. The following day, the convention announced that the monarchy was finished. France was now a **republic**.

CHAPTER 3

REIGN OF TERROR

The ranks of the French military were greatly increased after the country became a republic.

THE VICTORY AT VALMY AND the founding of the republic sent a surge of revolutionary spirit and national pride through France's population. As a result, enlistment in the French military soared. Beginning in the fall of 1792, French troops pushed toward Austria and Belgium. The military regained the territory it had lost in the early part of the war and expanded its reach into neighboring countries.

A Convention Divided

At the same time, a rift was widening between two factions in the National Convention. One faction, called the Montagnards, was led by Robespierre and the Jacobins. This group wanted to focus less on spreading the revolution abroad and more on bringing equal rights and economic advantages to the country's lower classes. The other faction, called the Girondins, believed that the government should be led by the bourgeoisie. The Girondins also wished to continue spreading revolution by way of the military.

Robespierre delivered more than 500 speeches during his time as a Jacobin leader.

Both sides were pleased with the recent establishment of the republic and had no interest in bringing the king back to power. However, the Montagnards held much more extreme views about how to deal with the monarchy. Instead of allowing Louis to remain in captivity or leave the country, the Montagnards called for his execution. The group began to win support, and soon overpowered the Girondins for control of the National Convention.

The King Is Dead

In November 1792, government agents discovered documents proving that Louis had been plotting with émigrés to defeat the revolutionary government and return to power. This discovery verified what many revolutionaries had believed all along. The Montagnard-led National Convention agreed on December 3 that Louis should stand trial for **treason**. The king was allowed to present his side of the case in two meetings that month.

Though the Girondins supported the king during the trial, they did not have enough influence to affect the outcome. In mid-January, 1793, King Louis XVI was found guilty of treason and sentenced to death. The final vote was 380 to 310, in favor of execution. "Louis must die," said Robespierre, "so that the country may live."

On January 21, Louis was allowed to spend time with his family before being taken to the Place de la Révolution, a large public square in Paris. There, he

YESTERDAY'S HEADLINES

The execution of King Louis XVI was a major event covered by newspapers around the world. The January 25, 1793, edition of the London *Times* cast a critical eye on the execution, presenting it as an example of what happens when a radical revolutionary government is allowed to get out of control. The article describes the French government as the "most execrable [detestable] villains upon the face of the earth" and the execution itself as "the uttermost diabolical stretch of savage cruelty."

was beheaded by **guillotine** in front of a crowd of around 20,000 cheering people.

In early August, Marie-Antoinette was taken from the Temple, where she had been imprisoned with her family for the previous year. Officials locked the queen in a dark prison cell. While she was there, a loyal counterrevolutionary attempted to slip her a note about an escape plan. However, a prison guard discovered the note and passed it along to the Montagnard leaders. As a result, Marie-Antoinette followed the fate of her late husband and was placed on trial for treason. She was quickly found guilty, and on October 16 she was publicly guillotined at the Place de la Révolution.

Artist Jacques-Louis David, a Jacobin ally of Robespierre, was present at the execution of Marie-Antoinette. There, he drew a simple sketch of the fallen queen as she awaited her fate. See page 60 for a link to view the sketch and read more about it online.

Power to the Poor

In the spring of 1793, France once again began suffering a string of military defeats in the war against Austria. The French were forced back out of Belgium and the Rhineland, territories they had taken over in the months following the Battle of Valmy. To make matters worse, Austria and Prussia formed a **coalition** with several other European nations, including Great Britain and Spain, to oppose France.

Marie-Antoinette appeared emotionless as she traveled to her execution.

Back at home, the Montagnard-dominated government began to make big changes to the way the nation was run. In order to maintain the support of the working-class revolutionaries, or *sans-culottes*, the Montagnards began to advance a program of radical reforms to benefit the poor. They increased taxes on the rich while increasing government assistance for poor and disabled people. The government also took control of the property left behind by fleeing émigrés and sold it to people still living in the country. A free education system was established, and children were required to attend school.

Many people, including nobles, clergy, and some of the bourgeoisie, were affected negatively by these new policies. Once again, violent uprisings occurred throughout the country. This time, however, the government was prepared to deal with them.

La Terreur

In April 1793, the National Convention set up a new organization called the Committee of Public Safety. The committee was given the responsibility of overseeing France's protection against its enemies, both at home and abroad.

In July, Robespierre and several other Jacobins were elected to serve on the committee. Robespierre and his committee used their influence to take control of the entire convention. They soon began to eliminate enemies of the Montagnards and suppress the uprisings that had been taking place throughout France.

On September 5, the committee announced a new policy of *terreur*, or terror, on the government's enemies. In the following months, the committee and its Jacobin allies across the country began arresting and executing anyone who was believed to be standing in the way of the Montagnards' political goals. Between September 1793 and July 1794, at least 300,000 people were arrested. Many of them were nobles and priests who stood against the recent social and economic reforms. Around 17,000 of these prisoners were put on trial and executed. Countless others were killed without a trial or left to die in prison cells.

A VIEW FROM ABROAD

People in the United States maintained a great interest in the French Revolution. At first, Americans were happy to see another nation taking up democratic ideals and fighting against a monarchy. They hoped that France would prove to be a valuable ally.

However, as the revolution progressed and began to bring about radical social changes, many Americans grew skeptical. They did not want the more extreme ideas of the French Revolution to spread into the United States. When the French government began arresting American citizens who happened to be in France during Robespierre's Reign of Terror, these fears grew even stronger.

THE RISE OF NAPOLEON

At the Battle of Fleurus, French generals Jean-Baptiste Jourdan and Jean-Baptiste Kléber led 73,000 troops against 52,000 Austrian and Dutch forces.

ON AUGUST 23, 1793, THE National Convention authorized a *levée en masse* (military enlistment). This required all French men between the ages of 18 and 25 to join the army. As a result, the French military soon swelled to nearly one million troops. This rapid growth enabled the French to once again experience a long period of success in the war with neighboring countries. After defeating Austria at the Battle of Fleurus in June 1794, France was able to take control of Belgium once again, regaining ground it had lost the previous year.

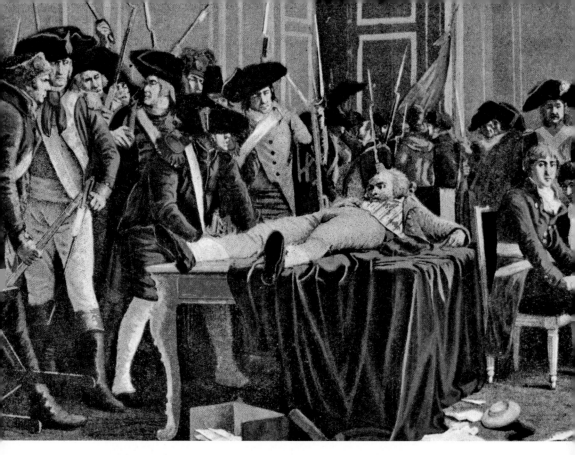

Robespierre attempted to kill himself just before he was captured by National Convention soldiers, but he failed, only injuring his jaw.

Terror Comes to an End

As France began to see success on the battlefield, things began to sour for Robespierre and the Montagnards. Public opinion of Robespierre had worsened during the Reign of Terror, and the members of the National Convention had finally had enough of the Committee of Public Safety's extreme behavior. On July 27, the convention voted to remove Robespierre from his position. The following day, he and 21 of his followers were beheaded at the Place de la Révolution, just as King Louis and Marie-Antoinette had been the previous year.

In the aftermath of the Reign of Terror, the Committee of Public Safety was reformed. It lost many of its powers to regulate **domestic** threats, and new, less radical, members were elected. Prisoners captured during the Reign of Terror were released, and dozens of Robespierre's followers were captured and executed.

Girondins in Charge

Yet again, the balance of power had shifted in France. After the Reign of Terror, many of the Montagnards were either executed or forced out of the National Convention. The few who remained had little influence. With the Girondins back

Maximilien de Robespierre

Maximilien de Robespierre was born in 1758 in Arras, France, where his grandparents raised him. He studied law and philosophy in college. As a lawyer, he specialized in representing poor people. This led him to develop a strong dislike of the monarchy and the system that prevented members of the lower class from rising in society.

When the government summoned the Estates-General in 1789, Robespierre was chosen to be one of the representatives from Arras. A vocal supporter of equal rights, he soon began to attract both political followers and political enemies. Though Robespierre is best remembered today for leading the violent Reign of Terror, he was also a key player in the movement to free France from the restrictions of the monarchy.

The Flag of France

The tricolor flag that represents France today was first designed during the French Revolution. When revolutionaries rose up in Paris in 1789, they wore the city's traditional colors, blue and red. As the movement grew to include the entire nation, they added white, which traditionally represented the royal family.

In 1794, the blue, white, and red tricolor design was adopted as the country's national flag. The flag represents liberty, equality, and other revolutionary values. Its simple, three-color design went on to influence the creation of many other new flags, as other nations of Europe replaced their traditional monarchies with representative governments.

in control of the convention, many of the radical reforms brought about by the Montagnards were reversed.

These new changes benefited the middle and upper classes, which had largely resisted the convention's previous changes. However, the changes once again left the country's lower classes to suffer economic and social hardships. Their problems were made even worse by serious food shortages in 1794 and 1795.

A New Constitution

On August 22, 1795, the National Convention approved another new constitution. This new constitution reorganized the government into two sections. The first was a parliament made up of elected representatives from throughout the country. The second was called the Directory. It consisted of five members selected by the elected parliament.

As with previous attempts to restructure the government, this new constitution did not please everyone. Royalists, people who hoped for a return to the monarchy, and Jacobins raised protests against the new constitution. One large group of royalists even tried to stage a massive revolt in Paris on October 5. However, a skilled young general named Napoleon Bonaparte happened to be in Paris at the time. Under his leadership, the French military easily drove the royalists away.

The Directory ruled France for just four years, between November 1795 and November 1799.

Napoleon's coup d'etat forced the members of the Directory to resign their positions.

Soon after Napoleon's victory, the National Convention was disbanded and the Directory took control of the government. Impressed with Napoleon's efforts at the Paris revolt, the Directory promoted him and began to consult with him often on military decisions. This new position gave Napoleon an opportunity to get a close look at the inner workings of the country's political system.

Napoleon's Triumph

Under the leadership of Napoleon and other generals, the massive French army continued to spread across Europe. In March 1796, Napoleon was named commander in chief, giving him control over the entire army.

Meanwhile, the Directory was failing to provide strong leadership. Financial difficulties and government corruption once again caused dissatisfaction to spread across the country. As a result, many royalists began winning elected positions. Napoleon, who opposed the monarchy, was unhappy with this development. In September, he sent one of his generals to stage a **coup d'etat** against the royalists. The coup was successful, preventing yet another rebellion from shaking the French government.

As Napoleon and his army continued to see success in battle and to spread republican government throughout Europe, his power and influence in France grew. He became a national hero and a symbol of the revolutionary spirit. However, he had only power and ambition on his mind.

On November 9, 1799, Napoleon launched a coup d'etat against the Directory itself, establishing a new government with himself at the head. The revolution was essentially over. Five years later, Napoleon would declare himself emperor of France, becoming far more powerful than the king had been.

A FIRSTHAND LOOK AT
NAPOLEON'S COUP

After successfully overthrowing the French revolutionary government and installing himself as the country's new leader, Napoleon wrote his own account of the coup. See page 60 for a link to read Napoleon's writing online.

MAP OF THE EVENTS

What Happened Where?

Paris

Valmy

Versailles   The Bastille

FRANCE

Versailles
Versailles was home to the Palace of Versailles, the royal palace constructed during the reign of King Louis XIV. The Estates-General met in Versailles on May 5, 1789, to begin the debates that would eventually lead to the French Revolution.

The Bastille
Originally constructed as a fortress during the 14th century, the Bastille came to represent government oppression to the working people of Paris. The storming of the Bastille on July 14, 1789, was one of the defining events of the revolution.

Valmy
On September 20, 1792, the French military scored a major victory at the Battle of Valmy. This victory inspired the National Constituent Assembly to declare an end to the monarchy in France, officially making the country a republic.

Mediterranean Sea

Only the Beginning

Napoleon became emperor of France in 1804 and ruled the country for the following 10 years.

With Napoleon in control, France returned to a state similar to what it had been under the monarchy. One ruler held absolute command over the nation, while corruption was widespread among other government officials.

However, the revolutionary spirit remained alive in France. Napoleon suffered a series of defeats by a coalition of European nations leading up to the spring of 1814. As a result, Napoleon gave up his place as leader of France and was forced out of the country. A year later, he tried to regain power, but a major defeat by the European coalition at the Battle of Waterloo in 1815 caused him to be permanently overthrown. In Napoleon's absence, the monarchy returned to France. This set in motion a series of revolutions and major governmental changes that lasted more than a century. The modern French government was finally established in 1958. Though it took time, the revolutionaries won. With an elected government, equality, and freedom for all, France now represents everything the revolution stood for.

Napoleon's defeat at the Battle of Waterloo put an end to France's long war against the rest of Europe.

TROOPS AT THE BATTLE OF WATERLOO.

Charles-Alexandre de Calonne

Charles-Alexandre de Calonne (1734–1802) was a government official in charge of France's finances in the years leading up to the revolution. His attempts to raise funds by taxing the country's clergy and nobles failed, and Louis removed him from his position in 1787.

King Louis XVI (1754–1793) was the king of France at the time of the revolution. His weak leadership helped spur discontent among the people of France, and his continued resistance to governmental reform led to his execution.

Marie-Antoinette (1755–1793) was Louis XVI's wife and the queen of France during the revolution. Because of her lavish lifestyle and uncaring attitude toward the country's poor, she was widely disliked by the lower and middle classes.

Marie-Antoinette

Maximilien de Robespierre (1758–1794)
was an influential Jacobin leader who
helped push a program of radical social
and economic reform. In 1793 and 1794,
Robespierre led the infamous Reign of
Terror, in which hundreds of thousands
of his political opponents were jailed or
executed.

Napoleon Bonaparte (1769–1821)
rose through the ranks of the French
military during the revolution. His military
success made him a national hero, and he
eventually used this power to install himself
as emperor of France.

Maximilien de Robespierre

TIMELINE

1774

May
Louis XVI becomes king of France.

1778

June
France officially enters the American Revolution.

1786

August
Charles-Alexandre de Calonne proposes his plan for economic reform.

1792

April
France declares war on Austria.

September
The monarchy is abolished and France becomes a republic.

1793

January
King Louis XVI is found guilty of treason and executed.

September
The Reign of Terror begins.

October
Marie-Antoinette is found guilty of treason and executed.

1794

July
The Reign of Terror ends as Robespierre and his followers are executed.

1789

May The Estates-General meets in Versailles.

June The Third Estate breaks apart from the Estates-General to form the National Assembly.

July Louis agrees to recognize the National Assembly, which is renamed the National Constituent Assembly; revolutionaries take control of Paris, starting with the Bastille prison.

August The National Constituent Assembly ends the feudal system and issues the Declaration of the Rights of Man and of the Citizen.

1791

June
The royal family attempts to escape France, but revolutionaries force them to remain in the country.

1795

August
The National Convention approves a new constitution, establishing the Directory and an elected parliament.

1796

March
Napoleon is appointed commander in chief of the French army.

1799

November
Napoleon launches a coup d'etat against the Directory, installing himself as the head of the government.

LIVING HISTORY

Primary sources provide firsthand evidence about a topic. Witnesses to a historical event create primary sources. They include autobiographies, newspaper reports of the time, oral histories, photographs, and memoirs. A secondary source analyzes primary sources and is one step or more removed from the event. Secondary sources include textbooks, encyclopedias, and commentaries. To view the following primary and secondary sources, go to www.factsfornow.scholastic.com. Enter the keywords **French Revolution** and look for the Living History logo Σ¡.

Σ¡ The Declaration of the Rights of Man and of the Citizen

In 1789, the National Constituent Assembly drew up a document to outline the principles of the revolution. The resulting Declaration of the Rights of Man and of the Citizen guarantees freedom and equality for all French citizens, among many other rights.

Σ¡ The Execution of Marie-Antoinette

Jacques-Louis David was one of the most respected artists in France at the time of the revolution. David was present at the execution of Marie-Antoinette and drew a simple sketch of the queen as she waited to face the guillotine.

Σ¡ Marie-Antoinette's Letter

Marie-Antoinette stayed in touch with her family by writing letters. In a June 14, 1773, letter to her mother, she writes of seeing poor people throughout Paris.

Σ¡ Napoleon's Coup

Napoleon's 1799 coup d'etat against the Directory gave him full control of the nation's government. Though Napoleon claims, in his account, to have only the nation's interests at heart, his actions were actually driven by his extreme ambition.

RESOURCES

Books

Heuston, Kimberley. *Napoleon: Emperor and Conqueror.* New York: Franklin Watts, 2010.

Schwartz, Heather. *The French Revolution: Terror and Triumph.* Huntington Beach, CA: Teacher Created Materials, 2012.

Schwartz, Heather. *Marie Antoinette: Controversial Queen of France.* Huntington Beach, CA: Teacher Created Materials, 2012.

Sonneborn, Liz. *France.* New York: Children's Press, 2013.

Visit this Scholastic Web site for more information on the French Revolution:
www.factsfornow.scholastic.com
Enter the keywords **French Revolution**

GLOSSARY

clergy (KLUR-jee) a group of religious officials, such as priests, ministers, and rabbis, who lead religious services

coalition (koh-uh-LISH-uhn) a group of allied forces

constitution (kahn-sti-TOO-shuhn) the basic laws of a country that state the rights of the people and the powers of the government

coup d'etat (KOO day-TAH) a movement to overthrow a government

domestic (duh-MES-tik) having to do with or within your own country

economic (ee-kuh-NAH-mihk) relating to the system of producing, distributing, and consuming goods and services

empires (EM-pirez) groups of countries or states that have the same ruler

feudalism (FYOO-duhl-iz-uhm) a medieval arrangement in which a lord gave people land and protection, and in return they had to work and fight for him

guillotine (GEE-uh-teen) a large machine with a sharp blade that slides down a frame, used to cut off the heads of criminals

monarchy (MAH-nur-key) a government in which the head of state is a king or queen

radical (RAD-i-kuhl) favoring extreme changes in existing views, habits, conditions, or institutions

republic (ri-PUHB-lik) a form of government in which the people have the power to elect representatives who manage the government

treason (TREE-zuhn) crime against one's own government

veto (VEE-toh) ability to stop a bill from becoming law

INDEX

Page numbers in *italics* indicate illustrations.

ABOUT THE AUTHOR

Josh Gregory writes and edits books for kids. He lives in Chicago, Illinois.